ROGUE SOLDIER
ONE MAN'S WAR

HE WASN'T ONE OF THEIR OWN, but the Condors of C Troop understood the guy in the black and drab "tiger suit" fatigues favored by the Special Forces had their commanding officer's approval to fly with them, so they took him along.

They knew him only as Staff Sergeant Keith, but word had it the slim, dark-haired young man with spectacles as thick as Coke bottle bottoms wasn't really an enlisted man at all, maybe not even Army. Some speculated he worked for the CIA. He was definitely some kind of spook gathering intelligence, but the Condors didn't challenge him. They needed all the help they could get.

Their mission was tough. They didn't realize it at the time, but they had just jumped into what would turn out to be the most intensive helicopter warfare ever. C Troop, 2nd of the 17th Cavalry, 101st Airborne Division, lost more men and aircraft in a month than they had since the Battle of Hamburger Hill, soon after the unit arrived in Vietnam two years earlier.

Staff Sergeant Ed Keith in Special Forces "tiger suit" fatigues
(Doug Bonnot collection)

By early February 1971, they were flying dozens of missions a day across the border into Laos in an audacious attempt late in the war to cut North Vietnam's principal supply route to the South. President Richard Nixon and his trusted national security adviser, Henry Kissinger, hoped the joint operation by South Vietnamese ground forces and U.S. helicopters, warplanes, and artillery would weaken the North Vietnamese enough to slow the fighting. Nixon had a re-election campaign coming up, and the increasingly unpopular war in Vietnam was dragging him down.

Now, after four weeks, the brazen drive to cut the Ho Chi Minh Trail was on the verge of debacle. South Vietnam's top divisions had bogged down and were being mercilessly pounded by enemy artillery and ground attacks. American helicopters carrying the South Vietnamese troops into battle, replenishing their ammunition and supplies and evacuating their wounded flew through a hail of ground fire to get in and out—and often didn't make it.

The mysterious Staff Sergeant Keith loved it. He would show up early on the flight line at Khe Sanh, the Americans' forward base close by the Laos border and well within range of North Vietnam's big guns hidden in the surrounding mountains. Keith carried high-tech binoculars, a nonstandard automatic rifle, a pair of survival knives, and not much else.

He usually flew aboard the unit's command-and-control Huey with Major James T. Newman, C Troop's commanding officer, or Captain Dennis Urick at the controls. His job was to help spot enemy forces and sensitive targets, such as communications wires, fuel lines, tanks and artillery. Newman thought he was uncannily good at it most of the time.

Yet, in his first nine days flying with the Condors, Keith's ride was hit by enemy fire three times. He shrugged off the danger and believed his partial color blindness gave him a rare ability to see targets others couldn't spot, making him more valuable than soldiers with normal vision.

"We knocked out a lot of targets," he said later.

That was not, however, what Staff Sergeant Edward Fulton Keith was assigned to do. He had a particular top-secret security clearance and was under orders not to venture "outside the wire," certainly not into hostile territory beyond South Vietnam where he might be captured. He shrugged at the rule.

"I expected to die in Vietnam," he said. "I know it sounds stupid, but you could have a lot of fun in the Army in wartime. I wanted to be the best soldier I could."

For as long as he could remember, Ed Keith had wanted to be a soldier. The military fascinated him. He was a middle-class kid from a broken home in California who was fascinated by guns from early boyhood. His father taught him and his brothers to shoot a 22-caliber rifle at an early age. When he was old enough to volunteer, however, he got off to a rocky start with the Army.

Ed Keith, nicknamed Sonny as a child, on the fender of a family truck at about 2 years old. (Bill Keith collection)

Keith had done well in high school, was pleased to be inducted into an honor society, and when he graduated in 1959, he enrolled in Brigham Young University, following a Mormon girlfriend to her chosen school in Utah. Not long after he got there, he decided it wasn't the place for him, and he chose to chase his own dream. He went home and enlisted in the Army, hoping to go to jump school and join an airborne unit. He made it through basic and advanced infantry training when someone noticed he had scored unusually well on military aptitude tests. Keith said he was told an exam showed he had a genius-level IQ of 142.

Private Keith after enlistment in the Army, probably 1961. (Bill Keith collection)

The Army offered to send him to Officer Candidate School at Fort Benning, Georgia. He was granted a security clearance of Secret—between Confidential and Top Secret—to qualify him to become a commissioned officer. He lasted about three weeks.

It was 1961, when Vietnam was a little-known trouble spot with a relative handful of American advisers supporting the South Vietnamese government and military. The peacetime Army was not yet desperate for junior officers and could afford to be picky. Keith's officer-training class was restricted to barracks, preparing for Saturday inspection, when he realized he didn't have a clean uniform to wear. He was sure that failing inspection would get him expelled from Officer Candidate School (OCS,) so he took off running to pick up a clean uniform at the post laundry, about 150 yards away. He made it back in time, got into uniform and passed inspection, but the following Monday, one of the men in his unit turned him in for leaving the barracks against orders.

The commanding officer kicked him out of school for violating an order. Keith was busted back to private and sent to Fort Bragg, North Carolina, to be trained on the job as a supply clerk, an ignominious turn for someone who joined the Army to kill Communists. It didn't take long, however, for Keith to move up a couple notches on the career ladder.

The Army ran on paperwork, and its leaders were always looking for soldiers who knew how to type. When Keith's superior officer at Fort Bragg discovered he had taken typing in school—and had remarkably high aptitude scores on his enlistment tests—he was quickly transferred to headquarters and elevated to clerk typist, a job that landed him in an office, elbow-to-elbow with his superiors. Despite his ouster from OCS, he retained his security clearance, which proved invaluable many times.

He also managed to pursue the parachute wings he had joined the Army to get. Fort Bragg still had a jump school in those days, and Keith wanted to apply, but he promptly hit another obstacle. When he showed up for training, the sergeant checking out would-be paratroopers spotted a line on Keith's medical form that said he had failed an "AOC Plates" exam, a standard test for partial or extensive color blindness. Keith didn't know what that meant, but the checker told him it disqualified him from jumping out of airplanes.

The sergeant suggested he get tested again at the base hospital, and Keith went straight there, where he again failed the AOC Plates test. The young soldier was sitting downstairs alone, crying, when it occurred to him that he couldn't have a serious vision problem because he had been accepted for Officer Candidate School only a few months before.

He erased the notation in his record, wrote in "AOC plates OK" and returned to the sergeant checking trainees for jump school. The sergeant looked at the paper, looked up at Keith, looked down again and up at the hopeful soldier two or three more times. "If you want to go that bad," he told the recruit, "it's through that door." Keith qualified as a paratrooper near the top of his class and discovered he loved jumping out of airplanes.

Years later, when his vision from the air was critical, he came to think of his partial color blindness as a God-given gift.

Although he was assigned to a Special Forces unit, Keith had not been trained to serve in the elite counter-insurgency force known for its rigorous training and the distinctive green berets worn by its troops.

His clerk-typist job was in the John F. Kennedy Special Warfare Center and School at Fort Bragg, where the Green Berets did their training, but he technically wasn't Special Forces-qualified, which limited his future assignments. He was working for a lieutenant colonel who had been to Vietnam as a military advisor and thought Keith was worth keeping, but there was only one slot open that would enable the enlisted man to keep his monthly bonus as a paratrooper. It was a vacancy for a weapons instructor, so Keith, who had only been trained to handle assault rifles and light weapons carried by infantrymen, taught Vietnam-bound Special Forces troops, including senior officers, to handle a broad range of weapons. The kid who grew up loving guns did just fine.

What he wanted, though, was to go to Okinawa, where the 1st Special Forces Group was sending counter-insurgency advisors to Vietnam to help the South Vietnamese regime beat back guerrilla fighters linked to the Communist North. He figured the war was bound to heat up, and he wanted to get in the fight. But there were no openings, and the ambitious, newly promoted buck sergeant decided to leave the Army and go back to school, this time to College of the Sequoias, a community college in Visalia, California, where Keith had been raised. He thought more education could get him another chance at being an officer and found he liked school, especially studying history. He read incessantly and remembered well. However, his second attempt at a college career didn't last.

Barely a year after he had left the Army, a Special Forces camp in South Vietnam, near the Laos border, was attacked and very nearly overrun by Viet Cong and North Vietnamese fighters on July 6, 1964. Master Sergeant Gabriel "Pop" Alamo, whom Keith liked and admired as a senior instructor when they were in the same training unit at Fort Bragg, was killed in the battle, and the detachment commander, Captain Roger Donlon, was awarded the first Medal of Honor to go to a Green Beret and the first to an American in Vietnam. Keith was moved by the loss of a friend, but that wasn't all. He also interpreted President Lyndon Johnson's grant of the nation's highest award for combat valor to a soldier in Vietnam as a sign the war was heating up and U.S. involvement was bound to escalate. His hunch was right.

Keith went to an Army recruiter in Fresno and said he wanted to reenlist.

He was told he had been a civilian for fourteen months and was no longer eligible to reclaim his previous rank when he reenlisted. He gave up two of the three stripes he had worn on his arm and returned as a private first class. This time, he requested and was sent to the Army's intelligence school at Fort Devens in Massachusetts, because he thought he could do more important work as a spook than carrying a rifle in an airborne infantry unit. He qualified near the top of his class and was made a "traffic analyst," which meant he collected raw information from units in the field and decided where to send it.

With his new specialty came orders for Okinawa, this time to work at Torii Station, a secretive outfit that vacuumed up radio messages and other intelligence about Vietnam and tried to figure out what was happening in the little-understood conflict in Southeast Asia.

"I loved it there," Keith said years later. "I became extremely good at what I did." To get better still, he re-enlisted in 1966, promising the Army he would stay for six years if it would send him to language school. The buildup of U.S. forces in Vietnam was underway, but Keith was told he was needed for an operation in a remote area of Pakistan, from which he would spy on the Chinese. He expected to live in camps, moving frequently to set up antennas to search for the best listening posts that could pick up transmissions from China. He studied Mandarin, the official language of China that in those days was a key sponsor of its fellow Communist regime in North Vietnam. From then on, Keith worked for a shadowy organization that called itself the Army Security Agency.

The little-known agency was set up at the end of World War II to gather "signals intelligence," information of military importance transmitted by radio, telephone, telegraph or other electronic means. It answered to the National Security Agency, and its existence was rarely mentioned publicly. In the early days of U.S. involvement in Vietnam, members of ASA set up operations in South Vietnam identifying themselves as Radio Research units to conceal their actual lineage. As the war escalated and hundreds of thousands of American soldiers entered the war zone, Radio Research troops were attached to combat units to inform unit commanders of enemy activity around them, but they continued to report to the NSA and ASA through intelligence channels as well. Some Radio Research members learned to exploit the system by playing one set of bosses against the other.

Keith, however, wasn't sent to Vietnam after language school in Monterey,

California. He was ordered back to Okinawa to work with a special operations detachment analyzing incoming Morse code that Army "clackers" recorded by listening to radio broadcasts and jotting down the letters being transmitted as dots and dashes. Analysts with language training, like Keith, would study the code, translate what they could and figure out what it meant. He was promoted to staff sergeant, E-6, and in early 1969, was sent to the island of Taiwan, headquarters of the Nationalist Chinese army that had been driven off the Chinese mainland by the Communists in 1949. The Nationalists, allies of the United States, were playing war games, pretending they were invading the mainland to recapture it from the Communists. Keith spent four months with them, then went home to California on leave.

His brother, Bill, remembers Ed's brief times at home were spent doing things he had been taught in the Army. Bill picked him up at a train station once and asked him what he wanted to do. "Parachute," he said, and they drove straight to an airfield, where Ed spent the rest of his leave jumping.

Another time, he recalled, they went shooting together out in the country. Ed had put together a sniper rifle that used 6mm, hand-loaded ammunition, and they took it to an abandoned cattle ranch, where they calibrated the scope for 1,000 yards, propped the 17-pound weapon on the roof of their car, and picked off squirrels and rabbits too far away to see with the naked eye.

During an earlier visit, when the family was living in Corcoran, a small city about 200 miles north of Los Angeles, Ed came down one Friday night wearing dress pants, long sleeves, and a sport coat.

"Where are you going?" his father asked, according to Bill, who witnessed the scene.

"Going out," said Ed.

"That's ridiculous," his father said. "This is Corcoran, a working men's town. There's nothing here to get dressed up for."

"Fine," came the reply. "I'm going back to the Army." He left and didn't return for quite some time.

It was during a home leave after Keith was in Taiwan that he telephoned Army Security Agency headquarters and asked for assignment to the 5th Special Forces Group in Vietnam. He finally landed in Saigon on July 20, 1969, the day American astronauts Neil Armstrong and Buzz Aldrin landed their lunar module Eagle on the moon.

Keith at Mai Loc, one of several Special Forces camps in the mountains west of Quang Tri, He had been in Vietnam nearly a year when this photo was taken. (Doug Bonnot collection)

Assigned to work from Pleiku, a provincial capital in the mountainous interior known as the Central Highlands, Keith was sent out to the Duc Lap Special Forces Camp near the Cambodian border, where soldiers in the field had found a wire strung across the ground. He quickly determined it was an enemy telephone line and installed a tap on it to listen in. Other jobs brought him closer to the action. He was dispatched to the Mekong Delta, also close to the border region the enemy used as a sanctuary in neutral Cambodia, and went looking for phone lines to tap down there. He was with a small contingent of indigenous fighters recruited by Special Forces when two enemy machine gunners opened up on his group. Keith grabbed his radio operator and jumped into a bomb crater half full of water. They heard on their radio that two U.S. F-100 fighter jets were coming in to attack the gunners, and when Keith saw the planes were dropping napalm about 50 yards away, he pulled the radio man underwater, and they stayed down as long as they could. The jellied gasoline burst into scorching flames on impact, and Keith said the water in their stagnant little pond bubbled around them. The shooting stopped, and the pair surfaced to discover the enemy gunners were no longer firing.

He loved the months he spent with Special Forces units and the mercenaries they recruited from indigenous hill tribes along Vietnam's border with Cambodia and Laos.

In 1970, however, the Pentagon ordered the Fifth Special Forces Group to return home as part of President Nixon's drawdown of U.S. forces. Keith still had several months before his tour was up, and the Army ordered him to report to the 101st Airborne Division at Camp Eagle for reassignment. He did and was told to find a bed and hang around division headquarters until a slot was found for him. While he waited impatiently to hear what his future held, he completed an exam and qualified as a full-fledged "Green Beret." He had won the right to wear the distinctive head gear and the unit patch.

Meanwhile, an acquaintance, Sergeant First Class Douglas Bonnot, heard Keith was at Camp Eagle and set out to recruit him. The two young men had met on Okinawa when both were doing signals intelligence work, and Bonnot was pleased to learn Keith was available.

Bonnot, who was at Phu Bai, only a few miles from Camp Eagle, was the noncommissioned officer-in-charge of operations at the 265th Radio Research Company, a signals intelligence unit attached to the 101st. He and Keith were meant for each other.

A career intelligence specialist, Bonnot bristled at what he considered his parent organization's rather academic, long-range view of its mission. The agency had been set up in peacetime to collect and distribute intelligence for strategic planning in preparation for future wars. In Bonnot's view, the passive agency failed to revise its approach when it went to war. He was frustrated repeatedly that solid information about North Vietnamese intentions was being picked up by the people in his unit, but the intelligence wasn't reaching troops in the field until it was too late. Bonnot's immediate boss, First Lieutenant Bruce Rollman, called it "the perishability of intelligence."

"If you can't get it to the guys in the field exactly when they need it, you might as well forget about it," Rollman said in an interview long afterward. But he explained that under the military's rules at the time, even if the Radio Research men in the field picked up a transmission and relayed it to the operations center at headquarters—and if cryptologists and translators recognized the significance and immediacy of the message—it had to be handed to a Special Security Officer (SSO), cleaned up to his satisfaction, passed along to the 101st Airborne Division's intelligence staff at headquarters, evaluated there and then passed back through secure channels to troops in the field. "By the time it got back to the field, it was too late to be of any use," Rollman lamented.

Bonnot also believed that his men shouldn't be kept away from action by restricting them to defensive enclosures surrounded by high chain-link fences and topped by concertina wire deep inside large, comparatively safe Army bases. He wanted them in the field, closer to enemy radios and telephone wires. Keith was thrilled to join him.

The commanding officer of the 265th Radio Research Company, then-Captain Phil Bernstein, remembered Keith's arrival at headquarters. "So Ed rolls in one day on the back of a truck" coming from the helipad. He was wearing the Special Forces shoulder patch on his fatigues and had with him a pair of wooden Army foot lockers loaded with gear. "He said, 'Captain, I wanna talk to you a minute,'" Bernstein recalled years later. "He has these two foot lockers, and he's got hand grenades, belts of ammunition, knives, claymore mines" in one, and the other loaded with automatic weapons and pistols.

The commander was amazed that Keith had even been able to get all that firepower onto a military base and into a helicopter without special authorization, but he was also impressed by the sergeant's background and figured he could use him.

"We went off to one side, and I told him I had a very weak lieutenant leading one of my platoons, and I need your experience to prop up this weak lieutenant," Bernstein recalled. He appointed Keith platoon sergeant for that platoon, set him off in that right direction and never saw him again in Vietnam.

"I was always looking for a fight," Keith said. He expected to be killed and "wanted to do the best I could before that happened."

Keith quickly teamed up with Bonnot, a sergeant first class, one rank higher than Keith and, as noncommissioned officer-in-charge, the effective leader of more than 200 troops scattered around the northernmost region of South Vietnam on fire bases and outposts controlled by the 101st Airborne Division.

It was December 1970, about the time Bonnot's radio monitors began picking up clues that the North Vietnamese were moving large numbers of troops into positions in Laos near the border with South Vietnam and around

Tchepone. Tchepone, a Laotian town 30 miles west of the Vietnam border, was at the top of the Ho Chi Minh trail network, the principal supply funnel leading south and east into the populated coastal regions of South Vietnam. Bonnot's intelligence analysts interpreted the maneuvers as preparation for a spring offensive against U.S. forces below the Demilitarized Zone (DMZ) separating North and South Vietnam. What Bonnot's team wasn't told and didn't realize yet was that the North Vietnamese Army was actually reacting to an intelligence coup of its own. The NVA had learned of the allied invasion plan for a daring attack on its supply depots and trails. It was setting a trap.

Bonnot and his people were correct in deducing something was going on behind the scenes, but they weren't told what. One clue came when the Army reopened the abandoned Marine Combat Base at Khe Sanh, near the border of Laos and just south of the DMZ. Under the noses of North Vietnamese observers hiding in the surrounding hills and across the border, engineers and advance units set about repairing the airfield that had been heavily damaged during the 77-day artillery siege endured by the Marines three years earlier. The enemy's big guns that had pounded the base from well-camouflaged caves were still there—but silent—as the base came back to life.

"Something was up, and we had been left out of the planning, again," Bonnot wrote later.

Despite the growing antiwar movement in the United States and a congressional ban on U.S. cross-border operations, the allies' top-secret plan was to try a "Hail Mary" shot that some high military officers—including General Abrams—said might even end the war. President Nixon sent his most trusted military adviser, then-Brigadier General and Deputy National Security Adviser Alexander Haig, on a secret mission to Southeast Asia to assess government and military leaders' support for the mission. At least, top U.S. officials told him, the offensive would lead to lower U.S. casualties. Nixon, already focused on getting the public's mind off the war and improving his reelection prospects in 1972, approved the plan.

Informed of the allies' supposedly super-secret attack only days before it was to be executed, the Radio Research boys scrambled to scrounge, repair and deliver radios and intelligence-gathering gear to forward fire bases. According to Bonnot's account in his book, *The Sentinel and the Shooter,* when parts weren't available, his unit resorted—without authorization—to cutting equipment out of other units' military vehicles, using bolt cutters as necessary, to supply its field units with radios, batteries, and the tools of their trade.

Keith was ordered to set up a secure communications link at Khe Sanh, which was to be the forward headquarters, although neither Keith nor others in the unit were told what was really going on. At Khe Sanh, Staff Sergeant Keith, the skinny guy with thick glasses and tiger-suit fatigues, quickly persuaded an Army engineer with a bulldozer to dig out a sloping, cross-shaped trench to hold a bulky radio teletype machine they called a RATT and other gear used to monitor, copy, and distribute coded messages. The bulky communications setup was used to link troops in the field to division intelligence staff back at Camp Eagle and analysts as high and far away as the National Security Agency at its secret base outside Washington. Keith arranged to make the space large enough not only for the secure electronic equipment but for sleeping quarters in the relative safety of the 10-foot-deep trench. He named it the Bat Cave, a reference not only to the Batman comic books but to the silhouette of a bat on the wing that graced a bright yellow circle on the insignia patch of the 265th Radio Research Company.

Forward headquarters of 265th Radio Research Company at Khe Sanh
Living quarters in bunker covered by sand bags, RATT behind bunker, and company intelligence and operations offices in background. Khe Sanh's red earth was notorious for its coloration of skin, fabric and just about anything.
(Photo by Bruce Rollman)

*Keith and Sergeant First Class Doug Bonnot (left) outside Bat Cave
at Khe Sanh (Photo by Bruce Rollman)*

Keith, center, Bonnot, right, and unidentified soldier outside Bat Cave at Khe Sanh (Photo by Bruce Rollman)

*Sergeant First Class Doug Bonnot and 1st Lieutenant Bruce Rollman
at Khe Sanh (Bruce Rollman collection)*

A few days after the invasion began on February 7, Keith left a couple of fellow sentinels at the Bat Cave and caught a helicopter ride to 101st Airborne Division headquarters at Camp Eagle, about 50 miles to the south. It was his turn for a shower, a hot meal, and a good night's rest. The 29-year-old soldier was asleep in a borrowed bunk at about 3 a.m., when a young private first class woke him with an order to carry a classified message to a general at Khe Sanh immediately.

The duty officer ordered a Huey helicopter and stood up a crew to fly Keith and his top-secret message to Brigadier General Olin E. Smith, an assistant division commander of the 101st Airborne "Screaming Eagles." Before Keith rushed off, a colonel determined that Smith was actually spending the night at Quang Tri, a larger American base somewhat closer to Camp Eagle and also engaged in support of the invasion force.

The landing zone at Eagle, however, was socked in by fog, and the pilot said it wasn't safe to fly. Hueys in those days rarely flew at night in the mountainous terrain, and the flight crews had limited experience flying by instruments only. Their electronics were still fairly primitive in those days. The PFC, carrying out orders from Bonnot's Radio Research team, insisted the message for the general was too urgent to wait, and the pilots told Keith to buckle in and they'd do their best but didn't know where or how they were going to land. The Huey lifted straight up, trying to get above the fog, and turned north, following the country's main highway, a two-lane road known as Q.L. 1, picking out any lights the crew could spot from the air. Tiny hamlets dotted the terrain along the highway, and some produced enough light to guide the uncertain flight crew heading north toward the DMZ.

When they reached Quang Tri, the crew spotted a brighter light that turned out to be the control tower of the base's airfield. They had made it.

Once on the ground, Keith was directed to a clutch of mobile-home trailers that constituted the general officers' quarters near the operations center. Keith knocked on a door and woke up a general—the wrong one as it turned out.

Lowly enlisted men rarely laid eyes on general officers—the ones with stars on their collars—and most were terrified in the presence of the military demigods. Keith, however, simply told the sleepy officer he had an urgent message for General Smith. The man he had awakened identified himself as Lieutenant General James W. Sutherland, a three-star and commander of all U.S. forces in the northernmost quarter of the country known as I (pronounced "eye") Corps. Smith, who had only recently been awarded his first star, was next door, so Keith woke him up and delivered the 24-page intelligence report.

The general asked the sergeant if he had read it, and Keith acknowledged that he had. The intelligence had come from a North Vietnamese radio transmission intercepted by the Radio Research team and translated that night to deliver to the top brass. The staff sergeant said the document, which was declassified years later, disclosed that the North Vietnamese knew in advance that American ground forces were not to cross the Laotian border and would only provide support to the South Vietnamese invaders. It also disclosed that the NVA intended to mass their own forces inside Laos to wait until the South Vietnamese infantry and armor had driven well into Laos, then cut them off and chew them up before they could get back to their bases in South Vietnam. That is, in fact, what happened in the coming weeks.

Keith recounted later that Smith read the report to himself and talked about it with the enlisted intelligence analyst before a meeting that morning with General Creighton Abrams, the overall commander of U.S. forces in Vietnam, who flew up from Saigon to discuss the fresh intelligence about the enemy's intentions. Abrams brought another four-star with him, General Lucius Clay Jr., commander of the U.S. 7th Air Force headquartered in Saigon. Keith, the messenger, lay down on the grass outside the generals' briefing room and got some sleep.

When the meeting was over, Smith offered to fly Keith back to Khe Sanh, where he introduced the soldier to Lieutenant Colonel Robert Molinelli, the much-admired commander of the 2nd of the 17th Cav.

Keith said he told Molinelli he could be more useful to the operation if he could fly over the terrain in Laos and help spot the enemy. Molinelli said he couldn't take him aboard his own command ship but turned him over to Major Jim Newman, commander of his squadron's C Troop, known as the Condors. Newman was quickly becoming a legend in the air cavalry for his daring exploits, particularly in rescuing downed helicopter crews under devastating enemy fire.

On the fourth day of the Laos operation, C Troop lost two Cobra gunships. Chief Warrant Officer Mickey McLeod and his newbie frontseater, Captain Clyde Wilkinson, dove on a North Vietnamese machine gun that fired at the little scout helicopter they were covering. Their gunship was picked off by an unseen machine gun camouflaged nearby. The aircraft drove straight into the ground and exploded, killing both crewmen.

Captain Jim Kane, flying another Cobra with Warrant Officer Jim Casher in the front seat, spotted the muzzle flashes of the enemy machine gun that killed their fellow crewmen and went for it with rockets fired from pods on either side of the Cobra. The explosive warheads hit one of two guns they had spotted, but the crew didn't see a third that popped up behind them and opened fire. A round took out the hydraulics, and smoke poured from the side of his aircraft.

Kane barely managed a crash landing that wounded both crewmen, who escaped from their burning aircraft and sought cover in a grove of trees. Major Newman, flying his command-and-control Huey out from Khe Sanh to direct the rescue, caught sight of Kane and Casher on the ground and went for them. Without landing, he steered his helicopter into the grove, cutting off treetops with his rotor blade until he got close enough for First Lieutenant Ed Kersey crouching behind him to reach down and pull both men into the open cargo bay of the Huey.

A few days later, Newman flew through withering enemy fire to rescue the crew of a medevac helicopter shot down on a South Vietnamese ranger base inside Laos. The 101st Airborne Division nominated Newman for a Medal of Honor for the rescue. It was later downgraded to a Distinguished Service Cross, the second highest medal for combat valor. Colonel Molinelli wasn't kidding when he told Staff Sergeant Keith that Newman was the best he had.

The same day, however, the Condors lost another helicopter, a bubble-faced OH-6 scout, and all three members of its crew.

Despite standing orders that barred signals intelligence people like Keith from exposing themselves to missions that might result in their capture, Keith decided it was more important to help the Condors fight in Laos than man his RATT communications gear back at Khe Sanh. With Bonnot's blessing—but without telling their commanding officer—Keith took every flight he could get.

At that point, Keith and Bonnot were operating as what they jokingly called the 605th Mobile Guerrilla Force (Provisional), a made-up unit with a shoulder patch they designed featuring a white tiger and tiny, yellow, spread-winged bat on a red and black background.

605th Mobile Guerrilla Force (Provisional)

It was strictly unauthorized, but expertly embroidered by Vietnamese civilians who offered myriad services outside U.S. military bases. At a glance, it looked official. The 605th had only a handful of members, buddies whom Bonnot trusted to share the intelligence they gleaned with those who had the most immediate use for it.

The first time he flew with Major Newman, Keith recalled later, they crossed the river into Laos, and Newman got a radio message that a South Vietnamese ranger base was under attack and in danger of being overrun. Newman turned toward the base a few miles to the north, and the crew could see artillery shells exploding all over the base. Keith spotted the source of at least some of the enemy artillery, and Newman called in Cobras and Air Force jet fighters to take it out.

A few minutes later, with the enemy guns silenced, Newman turned toward Keith behind him and said over the intercom, "How'd you like to fly with us?"

"All day every day, sir."

"Fine. You're flying with us now."

Meanwhile, another Army intelligence analyst like Keith found a similar opportunity to get into the fight.

Marque French, a new arrival in-country who had been taught the North Vietnamese dialect, was sent to Quang Tri Combat Base, one of the core bases supporting the Laos operation. He was assigned to a Radio Research team but got there to find a ghost camp with everyone headed out to monitoring positions closer to Laos. Someone handed him a batch of old messages that had been intercepted but never decoded and told him to try to break their code. French had been trained as an intelligence analyst, not a codebreaker but quickly realized the messages were too old to be useful in any case. He had joined the Army right out of high school and volunteered for Vietnam because he wanted to get in the war and quickly recognized the handoff as scut work.

Soon afterward, French discovered a friend from basic training who was flying as a crew chief aboard a Huey in A Troop, 2/17th Cavalry, a sister troop to Newman's, that was launching from Quang Tri in support of the Laos operation. The crew chief, Jimmy Ashcraft, persuaded him to come aboard as a temporary door gunner, the fourth position in the flight crew. The door gunner on a Huey sat on the opposite side from the crew chief and, like the crew chief, manned an M-60 machine gun. Without asking for permission, which he knew wouldn't be granted, French agreed and loved the excitement of defending his aircraft from enemy troops on the ground.

Back at Khe Sanh, Major Newman told Keith he wanted him to come along to try to locate an underwater bridge the North Vietnamese were using to drive convoys across a river at night while remaining invisible from the air during the day. The bridge was thought to serve a North Vietnamese supply depot close to Tchepone, the Laotian town at the top of the trail network. They approached at about 5,000 feet, and Keith suggested they drop down to treetop level, turn sharply to the right and fly east across the river. During the descent, they started taking fire from a North Vietnamese tank that Keith spotted below them—moments before he saw and plotted the location of the submerged bridge. Newman called in waiting Air Force bombers that took out both the bridge and the tank.

Keith recalled that on subsequent flights with Newman on March 7th, 8th and 15th, their chopper was hit by enemy fire intense enough for Newman to make precautionary landings to check out the damage before returning to Khe Sanh. Although he was the aircraft commander, whose assigned place was on the left side of the Huey, Newman always sat in the right seat. He was superstitious because he had been riding in the left seat on his first Vietnam tour when an AK-47 round pierced the clear plastic "chin bubble" at his feet, tore through his ankle and up his leg, very nearly ending his flying career. On one of Keith's flights with Newman, a bullet again came up through the plexiglass on the left side of the aircraft but missed the copilot. It nonetheless did enough damage that Newman set the craft on the ground in Laos to check it out before heading back to Vietnam.

A couple days later, Keith was told to go out with Captain Dennis Urick, who sometimes flew a specially equipped "left bank" chopper equipped with a sophisticated antenna array used to locate enemy radio transmitters. On March 17th, however, he was flying reconnaissance in Newman's place. Keith almost didn't go on the mission because when he climbed aboard in the rear there was no wire to connect him to the aircraft intercom and radios. Urick saw him getting out and told him to take the door gunner's cable hookup, so Keith settled in at the right end of the long bench seat that ran along the rear of the cargo compartment the full width of the aircraft. He was carrying a couple of survival-type sheath knives and wore a camouflage bandana around his neck that was fashioned from a bandage taken from a first-aid kit. Urick remembered he also carried sophisticated gyro-stabilized binoculars that helped sharpen distant images.

The invasion was in desperate straits, and South Vietnamese forces on the ground in Laos were taking a beating. As planned, the North Vietnamese Army had let the invasion force land with little resistance, but five weeks later, the South Vietnamese were strung out and bleeding, trying to fight their way home. Among the worst hit was the 4th Battalion, 1st Regiment (4/1) of the 1st Infantry Division, considered one of the Saigon regime's elite divisions. When the regiment's first three battalions were ordered to withdraw, the 4/1 was left behind to fight a rearguard action and enable the other battalions to escape.

It was the unit deepest in Laos, and the firebase it was trying to hold was surrounded and being hammered day and night by North Vietnamese artillery. All the battalion's remaining officers were killed the first night, and the ragged band of survivors, led by a sergeant and linked to the outside by a single field radio, was desperate for ammunition—or a ride out.

American helicopters couldn't penetrate the heavy fire and lost several aircraft trying to reach the beleaguered unit and rescue survivors of earlier shootdowns. Captain Urick's crew, flying a Huey borrowed from another unit, was assigned to pinpoint the enemy's gun positions and direct Cobra gunships to knock out the artillery long enough for other Hueys to get in and rescue the remnants of the battalion. Keith could see targets on the ground but couldn't mark them and told Urick to go around again to help get a fix on the guns.

The crew chief, Specialist 5 Richard Frazee, saw the whole escarpment below them suddenly light up with ground fire as tracer rounds in various colors whizzed past the circling helicopter. On its third and lowest pass through the enemy fire, six rounds from a 51-caliber machine gun, often regarded by crews as as the Hueys' worst threat, ripped the belly of the helicopter.

A white-hot incendiary bullet tore upward through the sole of Staff Sergeant Keith's left boot, came out through the top of his knee, hit his wrist and shoulder, and cut his mic cord before it smashed into the helicopter's transmission assembly controlling the main rotor overhead.

Frazee was firing his M-60 machine gun from the left rear door when he heard someone shouting over the intercom, "Who's hit? Who's hit?" He looked down and saw his own flight suit and chest armor soaked in blood. His first thought was that he must be wounded. But he turned and saw Keith on his back in the cargo bay with most of his leg missing and a few white ligaments still attached to his foot inside his boot. He saw the tissues twitch and turn the boot around.

Keith, too, realized part of his leg was lying in the co-pilot's lap. He could see red warning lights flashing on the dashboard but couldn't tell how serious the damage was to the aircraft. Frazee couldn't reach Keith from his machine gun position because the webbing of the bench seat in the borrowed helicopter blocked his way. He unhooked his safety strap and climbed out on the skid to get around the seat, but every surface he touched was slick with melted fat and blood from Keith's wound. He lost his grip and thought he would fall from the aircraft but managed to hold onto a strut and pull himself into the cargo compartment where Keith lay on the floor.

The crew chief reached Staff Sergeant Keith and tried to stanch the bleeding. The two men later differed about how they got a tourniquet around Keith's thigh. Frazee recalled he reached for a tail rotor tie-down strap and wound it around the stump, but Keith remembered he had the large bandana around his neck made from a camouflage medical dressing and used that to tie around his leg. He said he used his sheath knives to twist the bandage tight and cut off the blood flow.

Captain Urick recalled that Keith gave him a thumbs-up signal when the tourniquet was in place. He turned back to the controls and tried to steady the ship with warning lights flashing and the whole aircraft vibrating violently. The pilot radioed his three gunship escorts to cover him as he hastily descended, calculating that if he lost power, he was better off autorotating—essentially gliding—close to the ground in search of a place to land.

They made it back to Khe Sanh, where Urick executed a "controlled crash" on the landing pad outside the aid station. Keith was hastily off-loaded onto a stretcher and rushed inside. When medics saw the extent of his wounds, a medevac helicopter was summoned to fly him to the Army's 18th Surgical Hospital at Quang Tri, where his leg was amputated above the knee that night.

Urick's crew was sent out again on another borrowed chopper to search for enemy artillery that usually started shelling the combat base at dusk. Flying at 9,500 feet, well above the range of ordinary enemy weapons, the helicopter's automatic direction finder (ADF) started buzzing, indicating the aircraft was being "painted" by radar. At that moment, the crew chief shouted over the intercom that he saw puffs of gray smoke by the tail of the helicopter. Urick pushed the nose down into a steep dive and fell nearly 5,000 feet before he pulled out, having made his escape from the antiaircraft artillery they called "triple A." Assuming the rapid fall and recovery had damaged the engine, the aircraft commander called off the mission and headed home to Khe Sanh once again. Major Newman told him to pick up another Huey, fly his crew to Quang Tri and take the night off. They went by the hospital to see Staff Sergeant Keith, gave him a black Stetson "cav hat," the unauthorized but proud symbol of cavalry troops, and a 51-caliber bullet like the one that took his leg. The crew dug it out of the shot-up Huey and attached it to a dog-tag chain as a souvenir for Keith.

Urick said Keith started to cry, which made the Condors feel bad, but Keith told them his tears were only for the camaraderie he felt for his adopted C Troop.

His only complaint was that his left leg was cold. That was the one he had just lost.

Keith, like many seriously wounded American soldiers, was transferred to military hospitals in South Vietnam and Japan for more surgery and recuperation before being flown home to the United States. His father received a Western Union telegram that informed him his son had been wounded but gave no details and said more information would be forthcoming. Ed Keith's brother Bill remembered his father went into a panic, not knowing how seriously his son was wounded or when he would learn more. Bill suggested he call the Red Cross, which he did, and the family learned Ed was headed for Letterman Army Medical Center on the Presidio in San Francisco. They drove more than five hours to get there, but Ed hadn't arrived, and the hospital didn't know when he would. They went home to wait, and their wounded soldier showed up at the hospital a couple days later.

Keith remembered those early days at Letterman as a painful time, in part because they didn't give him much morphine, but he was proud he could take the pain. He had major surgery to clean up the leg wound that had been hastily treated during the emergency amputation. There was more surgery to remove shrapnel from his arm and shoulder, and therapists got him up and walking on crutches soon after the operation.

In late April, Ed's brother Chan, who was working for the Baltimore Orioles baseball team, brought the entire team to visit Ed and his fellow patients at the VA hospital. Ed, in his hospital robe, stood up from his wheelchair with his bandaged stump prominently showing, and welcomed the team with hand shakes and broad smiles all around. The players visited many other wounded soldiers and autographed baseballs for Ed and many more.

Keith, with the stump of his left leg protruding from his robe, greeting members of the Baltimore Orioles baseball team at Letterman Army Medical Center, where he was recovering from his wounds
(Courtesy of Bill Keith)

Two-and-a-half months after he had been wounded on March 17, Keith was sent home to Corcoran, California. He planned to enroll in college at Fresno State that fall, but in June, he had a nightmare, rolled out of bed and landed on his stump. That sent him back to the hospital. The injury didn't prove serious, but he postponed his return to school until February 1972. In

December, he had renewed his acquaintance with a young woman he had met in 1963 as a friend of her brother's. They were married soon afterward.

He spent much of the next three years at Fresno State, developed an acute interest in history and read voraciously.

Keith didn't complain about it, but soon after the amputation he began to experience what is known as phantom limb pain, a well-known but little-understood symptom after loss of a body part. Once thought to be a psychological phenomenon, the patient may feel shooting, crushing, throbbing or burning as if it were coming from the amputated appendage. Doctors now believe phantom limb pain is rooted in the brain or spinal cord, although they don't know why. In Keith's case, a burning sensation seemed to start in his foot and spread up to his knee, often growing so severe that he couldn't concentrate enough to read a book or watch television.

He started taking a controversial prescription opiate called Darvon for the phantom pain and credited the drug with making it possible for him to function. But Darvon also was addictive, and he took increasing doses to get an acceptable level of pain relief. Ed's brother Bill said after several years it began to affect his judgment and demeanor.

Ed nonetheless remained active, especially in pursuit of military history, his greatest passion. A professor introduced him to the Battle of Cowpens, a brief Revolutionary War engagement in a broad South Carolina pasture, that turned the tide of battle and led eventually to British General Charles Cornwallis's surrender to General George Washington's forces at Yorktown, Virginia, on October 19, 1781, effectively ending the Revolutionary War.

Ed loved to drive, in spite of his handicap, and drove a Mazda RX7 sports car for years. He crossed the country several times to visit the Cowpens battlefield, attend Civil or Revolutionary War reenactments, or just to visit new places. Living mainly off his Veterans Administration disability benefits, he had a propensity for stopping whenever he came upon a book sale or second-hand book store and often returned home with a stack of books for his collection. If he heard of a Civil War roundtable, he'd go and sometimes was designated as an announcer at reenactments because he had such a command of Civil War and other battles.

He tried but never much liked the prosthesis the government made for him, and got around for many years with a pair of crutches he tossed in his car. Bill marveled at his brother's command of details, whether historical facts or instructions on where to find a book or video in his extensive library.

Another brother, Ken, was a stockbroker and thought Ed would do well working for a think tank in Washington. He lined up an interview with a contact he had at the think tank. Ed drove to the nation's capital from California, pulled up outside the office, looked up at the imposing building and decided he didn't want to work there. He turned around and drove all the way home.

Ed's tastes were not for expensive luxuries, although he loved the Mazda, but Bill said he never seemed to have any money. He spent most of what he got on books, videos and donations to many different veterans organizations.

His politics were staunchly anticommunist, and in his later years, he spent hours watching Fox News.

The Keiths' father, who owned a small trucking company, hired three of his sons, two of whom became executives. Ed worked as a dispatcher but said he got fired several times. Bill said his brother took so many pills at times that he couldn't keep track of what he was doing and just walked around as if he were numb. He got to taking as many as 20 or 30 pills a day instead of the 3 or 4 that were prescribed.

"He would get strung out on 'em and be awake for days," his brother recalled. That exhausted Ed, and he might sleep for several days. Eventually, he went to the VA and entered a detoxification program to break his dependence on the drugs. But when the pain got to him, he would start again in what became a vicious cycle.

Doctors prescribed various drugs, including antidepressants and sleeping pills to treat his post-traumatic stress disorder (PTSD) as well as his pain.

Bill blamed the drugs for the dissolution of Ed's marriage, although Ed himself put it differently: "She could see she was having to mother me more than help me get better … She was probably right." They had no children.

Darvon, which was the target of a 30-year campaign to ban it as a dangerous narcotic, was finally ordered off the market by the Food and Drug Administration in 2010, but by that time Ed had tried numerous alternatives in search of relief from the phantom limb pain.

Ed was no gourmet, but he loved to eat and patronized several sandwich shops to enjoy their specialties. Bill remembered that when they went to the big VA hospital in Los Angeles, Ed liked to go by the 94th Aero Squadron Restaurant for it roast beef sandwich. The restaurant is named for the first

American unit sent into aerial combat in World War I, which Ed certainly knew.

Despite his having had a sophisticated knowledge of radio and telephone technology from his military training, Keith was uninterested in the technological revolution that swept past him in the 1990s. A fellow veteran gave him a laptop that he never used. He had a landline telephone with no answering machine or voicemail and didn't much mind missing calls. He figured those who knew him would call back.

Eventually, the drugs—and perhaps age—took the sharp edge off his memory. He focused more and more on the prospects for another war like Vietnam and viewed China as the greatest threat to U.S. superiority. He hoped the military and political leadership in Washington would have the determination and persistence in future wars that he thought they lacked in his war, and he blamed them for losing it.

As he approached 60, he gained weight, probably due largely to his weakness for tamales and enchiladas, and he lost mobility, which only aggravated the increase in weight and a stew of other health problems.

He gave up the Mazda and bought an automated wheelchair van that lifted him from the street to the driver's seat. He got around in that for several years, then stopped going out much on his own.

His brother Bill and Doug Bonnot, Ed's war buddy from the 265th Radio Research Company, stuck with him throughout.

In 2015, forty-four years after he was wounded, a VA doctor suggested he try a new pill for the phantom limb pain.

"I'd started taking drugs within three months of getting out of the Army," Keith recalled. "I was taking Darvon and morphine at one time. I tried anything I could get—not illegal drugs, but anything they had that might stop the pain.

"I could still feel the whole foot. It was like my foot was almost on fire. It wouldn't kill me, but it would stop me from doing anything I was doing." The pain killers helped take the edge off, but the agony was always there. Sometimes he even thought he could see the missing foot, as the burning sensation spread up to envelop the phantom knee.

Keith blamed the drugs for killing brain cells and stealing his keen intelligence.

So when the doctor proposed he try something different, he didn't hesitate.

It was a generic drug called venlafaxine, which had been available since the mid-1990s for treatment of depression. It was not a recognized pain killer.

Within forty-eight hours, Ed Keith's phantom limb pain was practically gone. "I still have pain in the leg but nothing like i used to have," he told me a couple years later. "I wasn't really pleasant to be around. This has made life bearable....I am so happy about that."

Bonnot and Urick, who was piloting the Huey when Ed got hit, revived a campaign to get the former soldier the Silver Star they thought he deserved, not only for the day he was wounded, but for other missions that they said saved many Americans' lives.

When Bonnot disclosed his intentions in a newsletter that he wrote for veterans of his old unit, his former commanding officer was infuriated.

"I was Keith's commanding officer during the time he decided to 'go rogue' and play Rambo," Bernstein wrote me in an email, adding that Keith had "the assistance and knowledge of my former company operations sergeant, SFC Douglas Bonnot, and my operations officer [Lieutenant Rollman]." After hearing that I was writing about Keith, he told me he didn't learn of Keith's "unauthorized, insubordinate, and illegal activities" until after he was wounded.

The former commander, who left active duty after Vietnam but continued to work in military intelligence as a civilian and retired as a colonel in the Army Reserve, said he only learned the details of what Rollman, Bonnot and Keith were up to 47 years later because they had kept their activities from him.

"I would have relieved all three soldiers and sent them to higher headquarters in Danang for insubordination," Bernstein said. He also learned of French's escapade as a door gunner and apparently confused the roles Keith and French played. He demeaned Keith as a lowly door gunner.

He said in a later interview that he "went ballistic" when he read in the newsletter of Bonnot's new effort to get Keith a Silver Star.

"He wasn't supposed to be there," he said of Keith. "He wasn't supposed to be doing that work. That wasn't his mission." Bernstein's pique was tinged by embarrassment. He only learned his sergeant had been wounded when a superior officer at higher headquarters called him and demanded to know what had happened. When Bernstein couldn't tell him, the senior officer ordered him to show up at his headquarters the next morning with an explanation for what had happened.

"We had top secret, special compartment intelligence clearances, called TSSCI," Bernstein said years later. "We could not be doing the kind of crap that Ed Keith was doing. In fact, it was against the law, against NSA directives, Department of the Army directives, Army Security Agency directives."

Bernstein stewed about the Bonnot report for a couple of months, then sat down and wrote a letter to the Army's personnel chief protesting the move to award Keith a Silver Star.

"You don't award soldiers medals for stupidity and for disobeying orders and for being insubordinate—at least not in my Army," the retired officer insisted. Then he received a new issue of Bonnot's newsletter with photos of Keith taken by Marque French, who had recently visited their old friend.

"It broke my heart," Bernstein said. "Here was this old guy who had caused me so many problems: white hair, sitting in a chair, in ill health. He still had a glint in his eye." But after Bernstein saw the pictures, the anger went out of him.

"I don't give a shit," the aging commander told himself. "They can give him the damn Medal of Honor for all I care. Let the man go to his grave with an award. Who am I to stop him from getting his last honors?"

Bernstein said he destroyed the letter he had written.

The old Condors with whom Keith had flown invited him to attend their reunion in San Antonio in October 2017. Ed Keith, his brother Bill, ex-Lieutenant Rollman and Doug Bonnot flew in for the occasion, and the Condors welcomed the Sentinels from the 265th as comrades. Bonnot gave a talk about the role of the signals intelligence boys, and when he told the group the difficulties they had getting their live information to the 101st Airborne Division intelligence staff, retired Major Bill Zierdt, the Condors' first commanding officer, stood up and interrupted.

"I was the division G2 (intelligence chief), and I didn't even know you existed!" said the exasperated Zierdt, who served in back-to-back assignments on both sides of the divide between a cavalry unit in the field and its division headquarters.

He and Bonnot agreed the designated Special Security Officer, the person who stood between the 265th Radio Research Company and the division headquarters, simply didn't pass along intercepted enemy communications that might have saved American lives, at least not in a time or fashion that would have made them useful.

Keith, by now visibly overweight, sat through the reunion sessions in his wheelchair, beaming at the many Condors who came to introduce themselves, including quite a few who had never met him or flown with him in Vietnam. His brother Bill and the small contingent from Radio Research stood around him along a wall or pulled up chairs nearby.

Keith, wearing gifts from C Troop, 2/17, a Cav hat and a
51-caliber bullet on a chain around his neck, at the Condors'
reunion in San Antonio, 2017 (Photo by Michael Putzel)

At the reunion banquet, Urick and the Condors presented Keith with a new black Stetson "Cav" hat with with the shiny brass crossed sabres of the 2/17 Cavalry and his rank of staff sergeant pinned to the crown. They also gave him a 51-caliber bullet hanging on a dog-tag chain to replace the one they had given him the night he was wounded. It had been stolen while he was in the hospital. Keith wore the hat and necklace proudly, then and later.

Bill Keith said he'd never seen his brother happier.

The campaign to get him that Silver Star gathered momentum in the following months, and Bonnot managed to recruit the help of Keith's congressman, House Republican Leader Kevin McCarthy, a native of Bakersfield.

Bonnot had also won the support several years earlier of retired Lieutenant General Sidney B. Berry, an aviator who served as the effective division commander of the 101st during the Laos operation in which Keith was wounded.

"Your decision to bend regulations to provide 'highly perishable' intelligence to the 2/17th Cavalry during Lam Son 719 was exactly right," Berry wrote in a letter to Bonnot dated April 6, 2006, from Berry's retirement quarters in Kennet Square, Pennsylvania. "Professional soldiers must frequently stick their necks out to add realism to regulations and to assist fellow soldiers in the field."

"I applaud your determination to gain the well-deserved Silver Star for SSG Ed Keith," Berry said. He recommended that Bonnot take up the matter with the Command Sergeant Major of the Army, the highest ranking enlisted man in the force.

Several years later, as Bonnot staged a reinvigorated campaign seeking recognition of Keith's service, Marque French told Bonnot the award had grown in its significance for the aging disabled vet: "This is important to him despite his stoicism. I think it gives him a sense that the last 45 years of suffering and loss were worthwhile. Like you, I would like to see him have that peace of mind…. A little recognition is such small compensation but means so much to him."

In July 2018, a staff member in Congressman McCarthy's office told Keith by telephone that the Army Awards Branch had recommended he receive the coveted medal but still needed clarification of a few minor points.

Keith misunderstood.

"Michael, this is Ed Keith," an elated but always controlled Keith said in a voicemail message left for me on July 19. "I wanted to let you know that I received the national Silver Star today. I thought you were one of the first people that would be interested. As I said, it's Ed Keith, and I hope you're doing well. Thank you so much. Bye."

It fell to Bonnot to explain to him the next day that there were still some loose ends, a few details to be sorted out.

His friends didn't realize it at the time, but Keith's health was failing faster than he understood. He was making plans to join a small get-together of Condors in Las Vegas in October, but he was supposed to have all his teeth extracted and replaced by dentures in a procedure that kept being postponed.

After he left his apartment to keep the appointment, Keith fell in the street and was hospitalized. In the emergency room, he was delusional to the point that for a brief time he didn't know who he was. The medical tests, however, didn't show anything remarkable except that his body was low in some vitamins. His awareness returned; his mind was sharp again, and he went home to his apartment.

When I spoke to him by phone, he was frustrated that he hadn't heard anything from Congressman McCarthy's office about the Silver Star.

"I just hope I get it before I die," Keith told me.

A few weeks later, he fell again, and that time doctors identified the seriousness of his situation. Ed's brother Bill said doctors told the family that, although Ed was not a drinker, he had developed cirrhosis of the liver, probably due to the decades of taking Darvon and other painkillers. The scarring on his liver, in turn, prevented the critical organ from clearing toxins from his system. As the toxins built up in his brain, they caused confusion, loss of concentration and, eventually, encephalopathy, a condition that can lead to dementia, seizures, coma and death. Ironically, his and Bill's mother, Johnnie Roberts Keith, was admitted to the same hospital in Bakersfield at almost the same time and died on September 11 at 93.

Doctors said there was little more they could do for Ed and recommended he be sent home with hospice care to keep him as comfortable as possible. He died on October 4 of multiple organ failure.

Bonnot was still trying to figure out what was holding up final approval of the award. He suspected it was the lack of a recommendation from Bernstein, their commanding officer in Vietnam.

"The award recommendation has yet to leave the congressman's Bakersfield office," he confided to French by email. "It has been there for two months." Bonnot added that after weeks of discussions with McCarthy's staff, he agreed to make some superficial changes to the appearance of the Army's DA Form 638 entitled Recommendation for Award. He had submitted numerous sworn witness statements and signed recommendations but added a letter he had just received from retired Army Lieutenant General Richard Zahner for good measure. Zahner spent practically all of his 36 years in the Army in military intelligence, was a top intelligence officer in Afghanistan and Iraq and retired as chief of intelligence for the Army after helping reorganize the Pentagon's intelligence apparatus to deal with new threats, particularly from cyberwarfare.

Reacting to indications that then-Captain Bernstein's opposition had held up Keith's medal, Zahner said Keith's former commander was "out of step" with the Army's position on supporting tactical units with sensitive intelligence.

"His failure to endorse the [award] package "is yet more evidence of a flawed judgment that should be disregarded in every aspect by the Board," Zahner wrote. "He was wrong then, was wrong since then and is wrong today —period."

Bonnot set about gathering old soldiers from the 265th and C Troop to attend Keith's burial at Arlington National Cemetery that was scheduled for December 12, 2018. On November 21, the day before Thanksgiving, he fell off a ladder while cleaning the gutters at his home and was killed.

Keith's burial was attended by a couple dozen family members and friends, including Captain Urick, Keith's pilot that day in Laos, and another Condor, Ted Hughes, as well as Lieutenant Rollman and five fellow alumni of the 265th Radio Research Company. As they passed the "Screaming Eagle" monument to the 101st Airborne Division on Memorial Avenue, several of them knew to walk around behind the tall granite pedestal under the winged bird to see "265th RRC" subtly engraved on the back of the monument. Bonnot, who helped get the special recognition added, told friends the symbolism of its placement was "befitting a unit that operated in the shadows."

101st Airborne Division Memorial at Arlington National Cemetery

Stealthy engraving on back of memorial

Most of the same people and quite a few more ex-Army spooks picked up the sad task of planning to gather again at Arlington National Cemetery, this time for First Sergeant Douglas W. Bonnot (retired).

Old Soldiers' Farewell
Members of the once-secret 265th Radio Research Company and of C Troop,
2/17 Cavalry, 101st Airborne Division, offer a final salute to their comrade,
Staff Sergeant Ed Keith, at Keith's burial in Arlington National Cemetery December 12, 2018. In
photo, right to left: Dan Klem, Dan Altstaetter,
Bruce Rollman, John Mastro (behind Rollman) John Purgason,
Ted Hughes, and Dennis Urick. (Photo by Michael Putzel)

With both Keith and Bonnot dead, the campaign for a Silver Star apparently fell by the wayside as well. When asked about the status of Congressman McCarthy's effort to get Keith the Silver Star, a staff member in his Bakersfield office, Monica Martin, said she couldn't discuss the case due to the Privacy Act, but she confirmed that the matter "is not still active."

Staff Sergeant Keith never got the Silver Star.